Days Out in

Central Florida

from

The Villages

Gillian Birch

To Roger

My driver, photographer, navigator, chief critic, sounding-board
and the best travel companion in the world

CONTENTS

PREFACE

Living in The Villages, we are surrounded by some amazing natural attractions, historic homes and exotic tropical gardens. Central Florida is stunning in its diversity and humbling in its natural beauty. Those looking for ideas on places to visit and great days out will find this book an informative resource and an inspiration to see more of the local attractions which are just a short drive away.

From viewing nature "in the raw" on an exciting Ocklawaha River airboat safari to listening to the magnificent carillon concerts in the gardens surrounding Bok Tower, there is something to thrill every reader, whether you are a keen walker, amateur gardener, history lover or wine connoisseur.

This book highlights some of my favorite days out in Central Florida and I have visited them all, some quite frequently, as an ordinary visitor. Each destination has an informative introduction, clear directions on how to get there from the Villages, things to do, admission costs and tips on the best times to visit. Every great day out should include a pleasant watering hole, so I have also included some suggested places to eat, which I hasten to add did not in any way solicit my business. I have combined each trip with other neighboring attractions which can be included, to extend your day out in Central Florida if you wish.

Planning days out from The Villages with this book is like traveling with a knowledgeable and local friend, with advice and tips enabling you to get the very most enjoyment from your home in Central Florida. It is an ideal resource to turn to for inspiration the next time you have visitors and want to show off the beautiful location in which you live. Whether you are traveling alone, as a family or with friends and neighbors, you will be surprised at what is on your doorstep when you live in The Villages.

Happy trails!

What's What

Introduction: Each destination begins with a short description of the attraction and what it offers, to help you choose a day out that will best suit your needs.

Location: Full address, contact details and GPS co-ordinates make getting there very easy.

Directions: The easy-to-follow directions and mileage to the destination all start from the **CVS Pharmacy on 466 (GPS: 30.902, -82.002),** at 5208 East County Road 466, The Villages, just in front of Publix Supermarket. Directions and mileage are all calculated from that point.

Suggested directions follow quiet roads and scenic routes wherever possible, to make the journey as enjoyable as the actual destination. Most places are less than 90 minutes by car from The Villages.

Things To Do: This section gives a full and detailed description of what to do at the attraction, including guided tours, personal tips, best times to visit and other pertinent information for you to get the most from your day out.

Where to Eat: These are all places that I have personally experienced and would happily go back to. The businesses did not know I was gathering information for a book; I was simply there as an ordinary paying customer.

Cost: Admission prices and cost of boat trips, guided tours etc. are all correct at time of going to press in early 2011. They are intended as a guideline only and may be subject to change in the future.

Opening
Times: For seasonal openings and annual events I have
                 supplied general information and telephone numbers.
                 It is advisable to call and confirm details before
                 setting off, to avoid disappointment.

Nearby
Attractions: Once you have enjoyed visiting your chosen
                 destination, other nearby attractions are suggested to
                 extend your day or to include as a detour on your
                 journey home.

Days Out in Central Florida from The Villages

Kanapaha Botanical Gardens

If you struggle to keep your Villages garden under control you will appreciate the enormous amount of work it takes to keep the lovely Kanapaha Gardens in tip-top condition all year-round. For maximum color, plan to visit these award-winning 62-acre gardens from June to September when the blooms are at their very best. The magnificent water gardens, hummingbird garden, rock garden and bamboo stands are an absolute delight.

Location
Kanapaha Botanical Gardens are just north of the Villages, at Gainesville.

4700 SW58 Drive
Gainesville
FL32608
Tel: (352) 372-4981

GPS Coordinates: 29.612, -82.409

Directions from the Villages to Kanapaha Gardens
- From the Villages, head north on Hwy 441 for approximately 60 miles, passing through the small towns of McIntosh and pretty Micanopy

- In Gainesville, turn left and follow the SR24 (Archer Road) west for 6 miles then follow the signs into the car park at Kanapaha Gardens, on the right-hand side of the road

The scenic journey is 68 miles and takes about 90 minutes.

For a more speedy route:

- Join the I-75 and head north to exit 384

- Head west on SR24 (Archer Road) for 1.3 miles and follow the signs into the car park at Kanapaha Gardens

This is an easy one hour drive on the I-75 and the total distance from The Villages is 60 miles.

Things to Do at Kanapaha Gardens
Kanapaha Botanical Gardens was started in 1978 by the non-profit North Florida Botanical Society. It now includes 24 major plant collections which are easily explored along the meandering 1½ mile footpath. It has the largest collection of bamboo in Florida, an attractive butterfly garden, a medicinal herb garden (look for the root beer plant!), a rock garden filled with alpines tucked between the boulders and an extensive palm hammock.

In spring, the azalea and camellia garden is a profusion of gorgeous blooms along with the spring flower garden. Later in the year enjoy the magnificent rose garden, cycads, the carnivorous plant garden, shady woodland walk and the oriental garden. There is a delightful gazebo and plenty of other natural stopping points to allow you to linger and enjoy the butterflies, birds and wildlife.

The water gardens with their running streams, fountains and clear pools deserve a special mention. In the summer the huge leaves of the giant Victoria water lilies are said to support the weight of a child, although this is not something recommended to try!

Get some ideas for hardy climbing plants in the ornamental vinery which has passion flowers, jasmine, pelican flowers and other colorful climbers. Finish your visit in the gift shop and plant nursery where you can pick up reasonably priced and unusual plants which are ideally suited to the climate in Central Florida.

Additional Info
Note - Closed Thursdays

Where to Eat around Kanapaha Gardens
Kanapaha has plenty of places for picnics so bring your own packed lunch and drinks and enjoy dining al fresco in these lovely surroundings.

Archer Road has many chain restaurants such as Sonny's Real Pit Bar-B-Q, Outback Steakhouse and TGI Friday's. If you plan to visit Downtown Gainesville there are several excellent restaurants including Harry's Seafood Bar & Grille on SE 1st Street.

Cost
Admission - Adults $6
Children (6-13) $3

Opening Times
Mon, Tues, Wed, Fri 9.a.m. to 5 p.m.
Sat and Sun 9 a.m. to dusk
CLOSED Thursdays

Nearby Attractions
- Micanopy is a quaint old town with several antique centers
- Downtown Gainesville has fine university architecture, theaters and restaurants

Lakeridge Winery

Whether you are a keen oenophile or simply want to see how wine is made, we are fortunate to have Florida's largest premium winery right on our doorstep at Clermont. Lakeridge Winery is open daily and offers interesting and informative guided tours around the vineyard and winery followed by a wine tasting of their selected wines. Even if you are not a wine-lover, you will enjoy the live jazz and the art and craft shows which the winery hosts and the well-stocked gift shop has some most unusual gifts.

Photo: LakeridgeWineries

Location
South of the Villages at Clermont, just off the Florida Turnpike.

Lakeridge Winery
19239 US 27 North
Clermont
FL34711
Tel: (352) 394-8627

GPS Coordinates: 28.630, -81.769

Directions from the Villages to Lakeridge Winery
If time is of the essence, you can zip down the Florida Turnpike to the winery (exit 289), and follow the US 27 south for 7 miles to reach this excellent attraction.

A more pleasant and scenic route is to follow Hwy 27 south from the Villages. Once you have cleared the traffic in Leesburg it is a pleasant drive which lifts the spirits and starts the day out in a relaxed state of mind. The total journey is 30 miles from The Villages and once you have crossed the Florida Turnpike, the winery's Spanish-style buildings and rows of vines are clearly visible on the right-hand side of the road.

Allow 50 minutes for this 30 mile trip.

Things to Do at Lakeridge Winery
Lakeridge Winery began in 1989 in an area that was once the center of Florida's grape industry. It is still run as a family business although the Cox family now employs more than 65 staff. Altogether the nine different wines have received more than 700 awards for excellence and remain very competitively priced. The winery currently produces almost a million bottles of wine per year and welcomes 110,000 personal visitors through its doors annually. The monthly events make every day out particularly fun, so check out the list of events below in the Additional Information section.

From dry white Chablis to full-bodied Cuvée Noir Reserve, Lakeridge Winery has something for every palate and occasion, including the celebratory Pink Crescendo sparkling wine and the semi-sweet Sunblush, for those who prefer rosé wines.

A good way to start your visit is by signing up for a place on the next available complimentary wine tour. Begin in the upstairs theater where you will see a 12-minute film presentation explaining the history of Lakeridge Winery, the growing of grapes in Florida and the wine-making process right through to the bottling and laying down of the wine. From the balcony there are some great views of the 127 acres of vines. Your personal tour guide will answer any questions and then take you to the wine tasting room. Enjoy an informative wine sampling of five of the winery's award-winning wines. You can learn so much about what makes wines differ in taste and how to choose and serve wines. If you wish to make a purchase, the wines are available by the bottle or by the case from the on-site shop. Allow 45 minutes for the tour and wine tasting.

Additional Info

Lakeridge Winery hosts some excellent monthly events from jazz concerts and art shows to the traditional August wine stomp! Dates vary slightly from year to year, so call first (352-394-8627) or checkout the exact dates on the Lakeridge Winery website: www.lakeridgewinery.com/aboutus-events.php

Monthly Events

Month	Event	Admission
January	Winter Music Series	Free admission
February	Winefest	$2 donation
March	Jazz, Wine & Seafood Festival	$2 donation
April	Blues at the Winery	$2 donation
May	Jazz on the Vineyard Green	$2 donation
June	Annual Harvest Festival	$2 donation
July	Summer Music Series	Free admission
August	August Stomp	$2 donation
September	Jazz at the Winery	$2 donation
October	Vintage Venture	$2 donation
November	Annual Holiday Open House	Free admission
December	Arts and Crafts Show	$2 donation

Where to Eat around Lakeridge Winery
Most special events at Lakeridge Winery include a number of concession stands which sell fresh lemonade, hot drinks and snacks.

Cost
Free admission and complimentary wine tours.
Some special events charge a $2 donation to specific local charities.

Opening Times
Mon – Sat 10 a.m. to 5 p.m.
Sunday 11 a.m. to 5 p.m.

Nearby Attractions
Combine the trip with a visit to Howey-in-the-Hills. The Mission Inn does a splendid Sunday brunch.

DeBary Hall

Those who enjoy seeing how the other half lived will enjoy a trip to DeBary Hall, a lovely Victorian mansion which is listed on the National Register of Historic Places. Guided tours of this elegant estate home are provided by local guides and visitors can then explore the grounds and outbuildings on the banks of the St Johns River.

Location
In the small town of DeBary, north of Sanford and east of Deltona.

210 Sunrise Blvd
DeBary
Tel: (386) 668-3840

GPS Coordinates: 28.875, -81.297

Directions from the Villages to DeBary Hall

- Head south from the Villages on Hwy 441 through Tavares and around Mount Dora
- Follow directions to Hwy 46 and travel east to I-4
- Head north on the I-4 for 5 miles and take Exit 108
- Travel west on DeBary Ave/Dirksen Drive
- Turn right on Mansion Blvd, left on Sunrise Blvd and follow the signs into the DeBary Hall parking lot

Allow 90 minutes for the 51 mile journey, and longer if you plan to stop for coffee in Mount Dora on the way!

Things to Do at DeBary Hall

Like many wealthy families seeking a warm respite from the New York winters, Frederick DeBary visited the east coast of Florida by steamboat in the 1870s. He had made his fortune as a wine merchant and was looking for a place to build a grand hunting estate and vacation home. He eventually acquired land on the banks of Lake Monroe and built this beautiful plantation-style home. There he entertained family and friends who enjoyed riding, fishing, shooting quail and "varmint" hunting. He also tried his hand at orange growing on the 6000 acre estate and ran commercial steam boats for a time, fuelled by the 19th century tourist boom.

Guided tours of DeBary Hall offer a fascinating insight into the life of the wealthy DeBary family and give a glimpse of gracious living in the period rooms.

Once your tour of this splendid Victorian Hunting Lodge home is over, head for the Visitor Center and learn all about the history of the St Johns River with an excellent film which includes a virtual steamboat ride. The film explains the role the St John's River played in making Florida accessible to wealthy northern families who built winter homes and estates in Florida in the 19th century. It also gives an informative look at the life of Frederick DeBary with photographs of DeBary Hall in its heyday with its fountain and exotic gardens.

Visit the various outbuildings which are put to good use around the estate. The stables are now used as function rooms but there are still restored carriages on display in part of the building. Peek inside the worker's cottage on the estate and see the latest must-have for Victorian homes – the ice house!

If you have any energy left, trek the 2.2 mile Spring-to-Spring Trail which starts at the DeBary trailhead pavilion. The estate also has a shady picnic area and a well-stocked gift shop.

Additional Info

Special interest tours at DeBary Hall can be booked with 2 weeks notice and are ideal for Red Hats groups and special interest clubs. Topics include an architecture tour, an ecological tour or a tea time tour, which includes an elegant tea-tasting experience.

Where to Eat around DeBary Hall

DeBary Hall is sadly lacking an on-site tearoom but staff will direct visitors into the small town of DeBary which has several restaurants and cafés. My personal preference is to head out to New Smyrna Beach (East on DeBary Ave and Doyle Road to Hwy 415 then north to pick up Hwy 44 East until you reach the beach, about 30 miles from DeBary). You can then drive south on the A1A and pick one of the waterfront bars overlooking the ocean or the intracoastal waterway for a pleasant drink and a reasonably priced meal with great waterfront views.

Cost

Admission is very affordable at $5 for adults, $4 for seniors and $2 for children 3-12.

Opening Times

Tuesday – Saturday 10 a.m. to 4 p.m.
Sunday Noon to 4 p.m.

Nearby Attractions

- Mount Dora
- New Smyrna Beach
- The lovely town of DeLand
- Ponce de Leon Lighthouse at Port Orange
- Blue Spring State Park

Cooter Pond Park, Inverness

This little gem was discovered by accident when I was traveling along Hwy 44 and the lovely fountain on the lake caught my eye. I have visited Cooter Pond Park many times since and always enjoy strolling the ½ mile boardwalk over the lake and the traffic-free walking/cycling trail which leads into the adjoining Wallace Brooks Park on Henderson Lake. It is a great place to take the grandchildren!

Location
On Hwy 44/41 as you enter the city of Inverness

181 Hwy 41 South
Inverness
FL34450

GPS Coordinates: 28.835, -82.328

Directions from the Villages to Cooter Pond Park
- Drive out of the Villages on Hwy 466 west
- Go straight across the traffic lights at Oxford and after a further 4.5 miles turn left onto Hwy 475. Immediately after the junction, the road crosses over the I-75
- Follow Hwy 475 around to the T-junction with Hwy 44 and make a right
- Enjoy the easy drive on this highway, past horse farms, lakes, developments, acres of farmland and countless oaks draped in Spanish moss
- Keep in the right hand lane as you approach Inverness, with the large Apopka Lake on your right
- Take the right filter lane at the traffic lights along Hwy 41 towards Inverness and immediately turn right at the police station into Cooter Pond Park. There is ample car parking right next to the police station.

Allow 40 minutes driving time to cover the 24-mile trip.

Things to Do at Cooter Pond Park
From the car park, Cooter Pond boardwalk is easy to spot. The boardwalk runs over the lake with several outlooks to view the fountain and the local wildlife. Hang over the side and in the clear water you can see many small bass and blue gill along with the cooter turtles after which the park is named. You may also spot the odd watchful alligator head if you look carefully between the water hyacinths, pickerel weed, spatterdock, bulrushes and other flowering water plants.

The lake with its lovely fountain always has plenty of moorhens, coots and pretty gallinules. I have also spotted blue herons, little blue herons, egrets, tricolor herons, hawks and rare limpkins on various visits. Follow the boardwalk counter-clockwise around Cooter Pond as it runs for about ½ mile then follow the grassy path around the lake for a further ¼ mile until you pop out on the paved Withlacoochee State Trail. Turn left and enjoy a walk along the trail to Wallace Brooks Park. If you fancy a rest with lovely lake views, there are plenty of benches along the way. Wallace Brooks Park has some swings and picnic pavilions and you can sit and watch the boats and jet skis on the much larger Henderson Lake. A further short boardwalk takes you into the main park itself.

You can saunter back the same scenic way that you came, or take a short cut. Take the road opposite the swings (E. Dampier Street) then make a left into Mill Ave, past some local houses and you will be back at the car park in less than 10 minutes.

Allow about 40 minutes total walking time if you do the whole out-and-back walk along the trail and boardwalk.

Additional Info
The Withlacoochee State Trail runs for 46 miles from Dunnellon to Owensboro Junction Trailhead/SR301 on the former railway line. Rumor has it that there was a derailment and a flat car and several box cars loaded with canned ham and ladies clothing sank in Cooter Pond. Some brave residents dived in to retrieve the goods but the large alligator scared them away. Some locals claim to have seen wheels and axles when the water level is low, but so far nothing has been recovered.

Where to Eat around Cooter Pond Park
Just across the road from the car park is the old district of Inverness around the Citrus County Courthouse with a variety of small shops, cafés and bars.

Cost
Free

Opening Times
Sunrise to sunset, 7 days a week.

Nearby Attractions
- Citrus County Fairground – rodeos, tractor pulls, flea markets and more!
- Brooksville & Weeki Wachee Springs Mermaid Shows
- McKethan Lake Nature Trail at Withlacoochee State Forest

Ocklawaha River Airboat Safari

Combine a thrilling airboat ride with the chance to see a host of Florida wildlife on a choice of splendid tours. Justin has 27 years' experience working with wildlife. He now owns and operates Airboat Rides Unlimited and takes visitors on eco-tours along the nearby Ocklawaha River. The airboat tours offer the chance to see Florida's pristine wetlands and experience incredible wildlife up close. Think "nature safari" rather than "airboat ride", although these ultra-quiet airboats do cruise comfortably at 30-35 m.p.h.

Photo: VisitOrlando

Location
Eco-friendly airboat tours start from:

Nelson's Outdoor Resort
19400 Southeast State Road 42
Umatilla
FL 32784

Tel: (352) 636-4060

GPS Coordinates: 28.995, -81.835

Directions from the Villages to Nelson's Outdoor Resort

- From the Villages, head north on Hwy 27/441
- Turn right on Hwy 42 and keep heading east through Weirsdale
- About 5½ miles east of Weirsdale, still on Hwy 42, Airboat Rides Unlimited is on the right hand side of the road immediately after crossing the Ocklawaha River Bridge
- Turn right into Nelson's Outdoor Resort Marina

What to Expect with Airboat Rides Unlimited

Justin has been working with wildlife in the local area for over 27 years. His exceptional knowledge and enthusiasm for airboat tours shines through as he introduces the wonders of Floridian wildlife to visitors. Each ride through the quiet backwaters is different, stopping to investigate sightings such as bears, herons, alligators, turtles, frogs and fish.

Choose from the various trips on offer, including moonlit night rides for optimum viewing potential. Enjoy the exhilarating ride high up on the airboat as Justin expertly guides the boat through the backwaters. Have your camera ready to capture unique opportunities to get up-close with these indigenous animals. Justin is happy to share his knowledge and love of the Florida outdoors with his passengers and answer any questions, making this a tailor-made trip which will be both educational and memorable.

Tours:

River Ride

This one hour ride is a great introduction to airboats and the Florida backwaters. It proceeds at a slow pace through the backwaters of the Ocklawaha River spotting large and small alligators, herons, bobcats and other Florida wildlife.

Marsh Ride

This ride is only available when the water table is suitably high. It is a 90-minute round trip through the wetlands as far as Lake Griffin, covering about 40 miles at speeds of up to 35 m.p.h. See deer, alligators, wading birds, sandhill cranes, and if you're really lucky, black bears, hogs and water buffalo.

River Excursion

Enjoy this 90-minute airboat adventure which covers around 40 miles of the Ocklawaha River and backwaters at speeds of up to 35 m.p.h. See big gators, gator nests, turtles, birds and other wildlife in their natural habitat.

Night Adventure

This 2-hour nighttime safari reveals a host of wildlife which can easily be missed during the day. Lights shine ahead on the dark water and pick up dozens of eyes warily looking back. See alligators, frogs, birds and mammals in these moonlit adventures.

Where to Eat around Nelson's Outdoor Resort

Nelson's Outdoor Resort has a small restaurant and shop for cold drinks, groceries, sandwiches and snacks. Try their famous pork BBQ sandwiches with homemade BBQ sauce or start the day with a full breakfast from the menu before your airboat trip. Indoor and outdoor seating is available at this friendly store and restaurant.

Cost

One hour River Ride	$25 per person
90 minute Marsh Ride	$50 per person
90 minute River Excursion	$50 per person
2 hour Night Ride	$50 per person

Reduced rates for children

Airboat Tour Times

Justin's Jungle Tours run 7 days a week, at 11a.m., 1 p.m. and 3 p.m. as well as after dark. Advance bookings are essential to secure your place.

Call (352) 636-4060 for all enquiries and reservations.

Trips are for minimum 2, maximum 6 passengers.

Top Tips

- Apply insect repellant
- Wear a hat and sunglasses on a sunny day
- Earmuffs are provided, but are not necessary on these modern super-quiet airboats
- Don't forget your camera!

Nearby Attractions

- Mount Dora
- Sunnyhill Restoration Area hiking trails
- Pontoon Boat Rentals are also available at Nelson's Outdoor Resort. Call (352) 821-FISH for details
- Alexander Springs

Bok Tower Gardens

One of the best days out which I can highly recommend is a trip to the Singing Tower and serene Bok Gardens. This National Historic Landmark offers beautifully maintained gardens, a superb bird hide, a historic home and the opportunity to hear a daily concert from the 60-bell carillon. These wonderful treats combine to make this a memorable day trip for gardeners and music lovers, just south of Orlando.

Location
1151 Tower Boulevard
Lake Wales, FL
Tel: 863-676-1408

GPS Coordinates: 27.938, -81.576

Directions from the Villages to Bok Tower Gardens

- Follow the US 27 south past Orlando. Continue for 23 miles after crossing the I-4.
- After passing Eagle Ridge Mall on the left in Lake Wales, turn left at the second traffic lights into Mountain Lake Cut Off.
- Turn right on Hwy 17 (signposted for Bok Tower Gardens).
- After 2/3rds of a mile turn left into Burns Ave.
- The entrance to the gardens is on the left after about one mile.

Parking is free on the shady car park.

Allow 1¾ hours for the pleasant 84-mile journey through rolling hills, lakes, orange groves and beautiful Florida scenery.

Things to Do At Bok Tower Gardens

Bok Tower Gardens offer 50 acres of well-tended gardens with year-round color and winding paths lined with azaleas and camellias, best enjoyed in February and March.

Start at the Visitor Center where a 10-minute film sets the scene for your visit to this unique National Historic Landmark. Enjoy the exhibits which tell of the life of Edward Bok, a Dutch immigrant who became Editor of Ladies Home Journal, won a Pulitzer Prize for his autobiography and worked successfully in the world of publishing.

Follow the meandering paths through the gardens admiring the labeled plants, flowering shrubs and the annual and perennial borders all enhanced by brass sculptures of Florida birdlife, actually created by Bok's President, David Price. Make your own discovery as you walk through the Endangered Plant Garden; take time to sit overlooking the pond in the bird hide known as the "Window on the Pond". Patience may be rewarded with sightings of a blue heron, jays, darting dragonflies, butterflies, gallinules and the colorful plumage of wood ducks.

Discover the greenhouses, the White Garden and the Japanese lantern as you make your way to the Singing Tower, built of pink marble and local cochinea. It has a stunning brass door depicting scenes from creation and at the upper level of this 205-foot high tower is the bell tower with a decorative design of open multicolored tiles. It is made doubly delightful when seen in the reflecting pool, graced by two resident white swans.

The land on which Bok Tower Gardens was created was purchased initially to preserve it as a bird sanctuary, giving migrating flocks a place to rest, feed and replenish their strength. This high point, deceptively known as Iron Mountain and at 300 feet one of the highest points in the state, was a favorite spot for Edward Bok to enjoy evening walks to view the sunsets from his nearby home.

Once he had secured the land he brought in the best craftsmen in the country to create landscaped gardens and his Singing Tower which was designed to house a 60-bell carillon.

The gardens were designed by Fredrick Olmsted Jr, whose father designed New York's Central Park. The tower was designed by architect Milton Medary, the sculpture was carved in place by Lee Lawrie and the bronze bells were cast by John Taylor Bellfounders in Loughborough, England and shipped to Florida. The Singing Tower was dedicated upon its completion in 1929 by President Calvin Coolidge.

The tower was built specifically to accommodate a 60-bell carillon and each afternoon at 1pm and 3pm a 30-minute concert can be enjoyed as the soft music drifts over the gardens. Master Carilloneur, William De Turk, plays a range of classics from powerful hymns and Bach preludes to film theme tunes and arrangements specially written for carillon. Few musicians in the world can play the complex carillon, with its many foot pedals and wooden batons which strike the melodious brass bells, weighing anything from 16 pounds to 11 tons.

Highlights in Bok Gardens include the Mock Blue Ginger with its magnificent blue blooms, and the Victoria water lily which has rimmed leaves more than a meter in diameter and huge blooms which open at dusk.

In the 1970s an adjoining property was purchased and added to Bok Gardens to increase the gardens and add a beautiful estate home. Built for the Buck family, it was a much-loved family residence, filled with European treasures and furnishings. It has heavy carved doorways and delightful views out to the formal gardens and fountain. Knowledgeable docents tell the story of the house and point out the details in each of the 20 rooms.

Where to Eat
The airy cafeteria at Bok Gardens provides light lunches, drinks, ice cream and snacks with tables overlooking the gardens. Step onto the terrace for al fresco dining and enjoy the scents of jasmine, tea olive and almond blossom.

Cost
Entrance fees are $10 for the gardens and the 30 minute outdoor carillon concerts near Bok Tower. Tours of the Pinewood Estate House are an additional $6. Free admission on your birthday – just show your ID!

Opening Times
Gardens open daily, 8 a.m. to 6 p.m.
Visitor Center open 9 a.m. to 5 p.m.

Top Tips
Best value if you plan to return to Bok Gardens (and you probably will!) is the annual membership.

Bok Tower Gardens has some annual events such as Boktoberfest, the middle weekend in October when entrance is free. Enjoy German food, beers, horticultural workshops and live music from a German ensemble.

Plan to arrive just before the hour, when the bells play an hourly tune. Choose a restful place to sit near the tower to enjoy the concerts at 1pm and 3pm.

Visit the gift shop and well-stocked plant shop which has many unusual plants which will survive in Central Florida. Take a little corner of Bok Gardens home with you, whilst helping support this very worthwhile non-profit attraction.

Nearby Attractions
- LEGOLAND, complete with its own mini replica Bok Tower, is opening close by in Fall 2011, on the site of the former Cypress Gardens

- Grove House on the US-27 offers tours and exhibits about the Florida Citrus industry

Blue Spring State Park

If you fancy seeing the amazing spectacle of more than 200 manatees in crystal clear water just yards from your feet, then head to Blue Spring State Park near DeLand. This gold award-winning state park is the winter home to more than 200 manatees which seek out the warm spring waters when the cold nights descend. The excellent boardwalk runs beside the lagoon with frequent lookout points over the exceptional blue-green waters. The Blue Spring Run is teeming with fish and in the summer is ideal for swimming, snorkeling, tubing, canoeing or taking a two-hour narrated boat trip along the St Johns River.

Location
Just southwest of DeLand near Orange City

2100 West French Avenue
Orange City
FL 32763
Tel: (386) 775-3663

GPS Coordinates: 28.953, -81.337

Directions from the Villages to Blue Spring State Park

- Head north from the Villages to Hwy 42
- Turn right and follow Hwy 42 east for about 45 miles, passing through the small communities of Altoona and Paisley
- At the junction with Hwy 44, turn left. As you enter the outskirts of DeLand, turn right at the traffic lights on Hwy 15 and travel south along Spring Garden Ave
- At the next major junction turn right (south) along US17/92 (S. Woodland Blvd.)
- Travel towards Orange City for about 3 miles then turn right on French Avenue. Blue Spring State Park is 2½ miles along this road on the left

Total journey is 63 miles from the Villages and takes just over an hour.

Things to Do at Blue Spring State Park

I have to admit I usually leave state parks to people with boats and bikes, but Blue Spring State Park caters admirably for those who want to amble around and enjoy the natural sights. This National Gold Medal Winning State Park has superb facilities as well as being Florida's premiere manatee refuge.

The 1/3 mile boardwalk runs beside the Blue Spring Run through a shady hardwood hammock. The natural beauty has everyone reaching for their cameras. Listen to the gasps of surprise as eyes focus on shoals of fish and the manatees, the stars of the show, in the clear waters below. The manatees swim into the lagoon in cold weather as the prolific Blue Spring disgorges 104 million gallons of water per day at a balmy 72°F. In contrast, the St Johns River, where the manatees feed, ranges from 50°F in winter to 80°F in summer.

Gazing into the spring waters from the viewing platforms is like gazing into nature's aquarium. Sunfish, longnose gar, tarpon, turtles and other water-loving creatures can clearly be seen against the white sandy bottom of the shallow lagoon. The waters are so clear that visitors can even see the scars from boat propellers on the manatees' soft grey hide. These gentle giants can reach 9-10 feet in length and weigh up to 3000lbs, which is amazing on a strictly vegetarian diet of seagrass!

For an even better view of the pristine springs and the wildlife, hire canoes and kayaks from the kiosk or book a three hour guided kayaking adventure with a naturalist/guide. If tour boats are more your idea of a day out, join the twice-daily trip up the St Johns River on quiet pontoon boats for an excellent two hour narrated tour. Every trip is different with alligators, fish, manatees, red-bellied turtles, wading birds, cooters and even the possibility of a black bear sighting.

Visitors can snorkel and dive from the swimming dock to see the source of the blue spring and the cave which goes down about 120 feet. Take a self-guided tour of the original 1872 Thursby House, the enviably located home of Louis Thursby and his family who settled here. A campsite, overnight cabins, children's play area and a 4-mile backwoods trail (each way) complete the excellent amenities. All you need to bring is a picnic and a bathing suit!

Additional Info
The best time to see the manatees is obviously in winter, from November to April, but here's a tip from a volunteer warden. Visit in the morning, after a cold night, and you will see as many as 200 of these endangered creatures that have moved into the warmer spring waters from the chilly St Johns River during the night. This is a sight few people in the world are privileged enough to see and future generations may never get the chance.

Where to Eat around Blue Spring State Park
The best place for a meal is in DeLand, the classy county seat of Volusia. Retrace your route but continue straight on along Hwy 17/92 (Woodland Blvd) to reach the center of Downtown. The Boston Coffee House on New York Avenue is a good choice for coffee or lunch and the Coffee Bistro 101 does excellent iced Frappuccino just around the corner on N. Woodland Ave. Main Street Grill is a local favorite for a meal and the Secret Garden, also

on E. New York Ave, offers a delectable menu of French and international inspired cuisine.

Cost
State Park fees $6 per car

Opening Times
Daily 8 a.m. to sunset.

Top Tips
Don't leave DeLand without browsing the lovely small shops and murals in the town center and check out the forthcoming program at the beautifully restored Art Deco Athens Theater, behind County Hall. A season ticket to the theater's first-class performances is highly recommended.

Nearby Attractions
- Downtown DeLand
- DeBary Mansion
- DeLeon Springs State Park
- Downtown Sanford and Lake Monroe

Central Florida Zoo, Sanford

The Central Florida Zoo and Botanical Gardens offers a great deal more than the 400 species of animals in naturalized enclosures. It has animal encounters and daily shows, a pleasant Florida Trek nature walk, garden features, a miniature train ride, Splash play area, and the authentic Battlefield Orlando Live. At the fantastic ZOOm Air Adventure Park, youngsters, teens and the young-at-heart can get harnessed up and navigate along zip-lines, aerial bridges, suspended tunnels, ropes, ladders and swinging logs which are spread throughout the treetops, high above the heads of other zoo visitors.

Photo: VisitOrlando

Location
Just west of the city of Sanford

3755 NW Hwy 17/92
Sanford
FL 32771
Tel: (407) 323-4450

GPS Coordinates: 28.857, -81.317

Directions from the Villages to the Central Florida Zoo

- Take Hwy 441 south for approximately 31 miles
- Turn left on Hwy 46 towards Sanford and continue for 17 miles
- On the outskirts of Sanford, go under the I-4 then turn left on Orange Blvd and follow it north to the junction with Hwy 17/92
- Turn right on Hwy 17/92 and immediately right again into the Central Florida Zoo

Total journey is 52 miles and takes about 1 hour 20 minutes.

Things to Do at the Central Florida Zoo

The Central Florida Zoo is not the greatest collection of exotic wildlife, but what it does have is well presented. A broad boardwalk links the various enclosures of big cats, reptiles, birds and other exotic animals. Many of the animals are on the Endangered or At Risk list in their native habitat. Informative signs mean you always learn something new. For example, did you know that emus can't fly but they are great swimmers? Or that big cats are found in all the continents except Australia?

Whoever added the 'm' to zoo to create the ZOOm Air Adventure was truly inspired. This aerial obstacle course of over 200 tree-top challenges is almost as much fun to watch as it is to participate in. In a separate part of the grounds is the pseudo Commando training area which is used for Battlefield Live Orlando Laser Tag – a sort of paintball adventure without the paint, using high-tech infra-red weapons.

If you want to stick to the traditional zoo, follow the program times to enjoy the various Animal Shows featuring birds, bugs, primates, cats and reptiles at various locations around the park. The shady boardwalk makes exploring the exhibits a pleasure, and on hot days kids can cool off in the Splash Ground, a play area of fountains.

Additional Info

Bring a towel, a picnic and a camera.

Where to Eat around the Central Florida Zoo
The zoo has an organized area with picnic tables. Cold drinks and frozen treats are available to buy around the zoo park.

Nearby, Downtown Sanford has plenty of coffee shops and restaurants along historic 1st Street.

Cost
Zoo Admission $11.95 with discounts for children and seniors 60+

Admission to the separate ZOOm Air Adventure Park ranges from $17.50 for the kid's course to $45.95 for the full 2½ hour Upland and Rainforest Experience.

Opening Times
9 a.m. to 5 p.m. daily

Nearby Attractions
- Just a little further east is the lovely RiverWalk, on the shores of Lake Monroe
- Explore the historic buildings in Downtown Sanford, many of which are on the Register of Historic Places
- Break the journey with a detour to Mount Dora or Eustis

Sanford Historic Downtown

Historic Downtown Sanford is a hidden gem in nearby Seminole County. Situated on the shores of the vast Lake Monroe which is part of the St John's River system, it has a mile-long RiverWalk with enticing swing bench seats beneath shady pergolas. The lakefront is just a couple of blocks from First Street which is well worth exploring on foot as it has 24 points of interest and historic buildings, many of which are on the Register of Historic Places. Enjoy Fort Mellon Park, the cafés and specialty shops before visiting the Sanford Museum and then finish the day at the Seminole Towne Center Mall, just off I-4.

Location
First Street/Park Avenue
Sanford
FL 32771
Tel: (407) 322-2212

GPS Coordinates: 28.841, -81.260

Directions from the Villages to Historic Downtown Sanford
- Take Hwy 441 south for approximately 31 miles
- Turn left on Hwy 46 and head east towards Sanford for 17 miles
- On the outskirts of Sanford, turn left on Orange Blvd and stay on it until you reach the junction with Hwy 17/92
- Turn right on Hwy 17/92 and follow the road past the zoo into Sanford, following signs for Downtown/RiverWalk

Total journey is 56 miles and takes about 1 hour 30 minutes.

Things to Do at Historic Downtown Sanford
There is plenty of on-street parking in bays beside the lovely Lake Monroe. The paved RiverWalk runs beside the lake for just over a mile, with frequent seats in shady gazebos. Relax on one of the lazy swinging bench seats if you get the chance. Watch the boat traffic around the marina and the many coots and herons at the water's edge.

The center of the Downtown District of Sanford is the historic clock on Magnolia Street. Stroll along First Street with its historic architecture and see if you can spot the following highlights:

- De Forest Block. Built in 1887 it is the oldest commercial building in Sanford at 121 E.1st St. It housed Touchton's Drug Store for 61 years and is on the National Register of Historic Places

- First National Bank building, Sanford's first skyscraper! Built in 1922, it still serves as a bank, located at 101 E. 1st Street

- Pico Hotel, built in 1887 to serve the passengers of the steamboats which plied the St John's River and Lake Monroe. It originally had a Turkish-style onion dome on the corner tower. It is situated at 200 N. Park Ave/1st Street

- Masonic Lodge, built in 1924, is home to one of the oldest chartered lodges in Florida. The cornerstone holds a time capsule at 212 N. Park Ave

- Rand Building, one of the first buildings to be built in Sanford after the fire of 1887. It once housed the newspaper offices of the Sanford Journal along with the early telephone exchange at 108 E. 1st St

- Milane Theatre, now restored and operating as the Helen Stairs Theater, this 1922 building has hosted everything from silent movies and Vaudeville to live performances by pianist Sergei Rachmaninoff, at 201 S. Magnolia Ave

Other architectural gems can also be admired on S. Magnolia Ave. Finish with a visit to the Sanford Museum at 520 E. 1st Street which has interesting exhibits on the history of the city and its founder, Henry A. Sanford. Admission is free.

Where to Eat in Historic Downtown Sanford
There is a good choice of cafés, restaurants and coffee shops in the Downtown District of Sanford including the Corner Café and Deli which is known for its Cuban Press sandwiches and salads; the ever-popular Hollerbach's Willow Tree German Café or the homely Colonial Room which serves American cuisine.

Cost
N/A

Opening Times
N/A

Nearby Attractions
- Central Florida Zoo
- Seminole Towne Center Mall, which is reached by heading west along Hwy 46 (W. 1st St) to Towne Center Blvd
- Mount Dora
- Eustis

Alexander Springs

Alexander Springs is an inviting spot within the Ocala National Forest with great scenery and a host of activities. The recreation area is set around the freshwater springs which gush an incredible 70 million gallons of sparkling spring water each day. Walking and biking trails, an interpretive trail, canoeing, snorkeling and bathing can all be enjoyed at this well-organized recreation area. On a hot summer's day there is nowhere better to cool off than at these pristine springs, surrounded by the ancient sandpine forest.

Photo: VisitOrlando

Location
Alexander Springs is in the southeast corner of the Ocala National Forest.

49525 County Road 445
Altoona
FL 32702
Tel: (352) 669-3522

GPS Coordinates: 29085, -81.578

Directions from the Villages to Alexander Springs

- From the north side of The Villages, head east along Hwy 42 to Altoona

- At the intersection with Hwy 19, turn left and travel north along Hwy 19, passing the Pittman Visitor Center on the left

- Turn right along Hwy 445 for about 7 miles after the Visitor Center and turn into Alexander Springs Recreation Area on the left

The trip takes just over an hour to cover the 39 miles through mostly rural countryside.

Things to Do at Alexander Springs

The 72°F waters at Alexander Springs create nature's own swimming pool, complete with gently sloping sandy beach. Snorkeling is popular to see the shoals of fish and underwater vegetation and scuba diving is permitted in the large spring boil. Facilities include changing rooms, showers and toilets. There is a kayak launch site and canoes and snorkeling equipment are available for hire. Following in the footsteps of the Timucuan Indians who lived here around 1000 years ago, the 1.1 mile interpretive trail along the boardwalk from the picnic area offers excellent sightings of wildlife along the Alexander Creek. Alligators, squirrels and birds all call this hardwood forest "home". The trail has two strategically placed observation platforms overlooking the lake.

Serious hikers can link up with the 66-mile long Florida National Scenic Trail which runs through the Ocala National Forest. The recreation area also has a cycle path - a 22-mile bike trail, marked by yellow diamonds through the pine forest, which makes a great adventure for non-motorized transport.

Where to Eat around Alexander Springs

The recreation area has plenty of picnic tables. At weekends and in the summer months there is a concession stand selling snacks, groceries, ice, cold drinks and other supplies.

Cost
Admission fee $5.50
Canoe rentals from $16 for 2 hours

Opening Times
8 a.m. to dusk, year-round

Nearby Attractions
- Mount Dora
- Airboat Rides on the Ocklawaha River
- Blue Spring State Park to see the manatees in winter
- DeLand

Brooksville, Weeki Wachee Springs and McKethan Lake

The day trip to Brooksville turned out to be totally different from what I had planned when I set off! Historic Brooksville has a few attractions but the nearby McKethan Lake and the water shows at Weeki Wachee Springs combined to make this a great day out. Take the scenic route - after all it's not the destination, it's the getting there that makes a great day out in Central Florida.

Location
Downtown Brooksville,
SR 50/Hwy 41

GPS Coordinates: 28.554, -82.389

Weeki Wachee Springs State Park
6131 Commercial Way
Weeki Wachee
FL 34606
Tel: (352) 592-5656

GPS Coordinates: 28.518, -82.575

McKethan Lake
Withlacoochee State Forest Visitor Center
15003 Broad Street,
Brooksville (Hwy 41, 8 miles north of Brooksville)
Tel: (352) 754-6896

GPS Coordinates: 28.647, -82.337

Directions from the Villages to Brooksville

The most scenic route to travel to Brooksville is west from the Villages along Hwy 44 to Inverness (about 24 miles) then turn left (south) along the US 41 to Brooksville. In more detail:

- Drive out of the Villages on Hwy 466 west
- Go straight across the traffic lights at Oxford and after a further 4.5 miles turn left onto Hwy 475. Immediately after the junction, the road crosses over the I-75
- Follow Hwy 475 around to the T-junction with Hwy 44 and make a right.
- Once you reach the junction with Hwy 41 in Inverness, turn left and continue until you reach Brooksville

Allow one hour to drive the 46 scenic miles to Brooksville.

Things to Do at Brooksville

This scenic two-lane Highway 41 runs through Floral City where on weekends the road is lined with flea markets and fruit stands. Enjoy the views of live oaks draped with yards of grey Spanish moss providing shade for old wooden homesteads. The route provides a wonderful snapshot of small-town life in Florida. Rows of mail boxes testify to the many small communities down each sandy track which disappear off the highway into the native Florida bush.

Historic Brooksville promises antebellum homes, specialty shops, cafés and murals with a laid-back atmosphere. Unfortunately the town has fallen victim to the out-of-town strip malls nearby and the general economic downturn. However, a drive around the downtown area will reward you with one or two charming mansions dating back to the 1880s and there are still several cafés in business. Look out for the huge, beautifully painted murals which are worth a snapshot, especially the Civil War mural on Broad Street.

The Hernando Historical Museum is housed in one of the lovely mansions, complete with gingerbread trim. It has a fine collection of 11,000 artifacts dating back to the Civil War. The museum is on the site of the Brooksville Raid and each year it hosts the largest Civil War re-enactment in Florida. The museum also offers two hour ghost tours at weekends with many tales of unexplained happenings on the property. Take your camera, digital recorder and EMF detector to record this paranormal experience, if you dare!

Weeki Wachee Springs State Park

Just 11 miles further west from Brooksdale along Hwy 50 is the Weeki Wachee Springs State Park on Hwy 50/US19 junction. It offers water slides, river cruises, canoe rentals and organized diving trips. And where else can you watch a world-famous Mermaid Show? Aqua belles have been performing enchanting shows since the 1940s and currently recreate the Hans Christian Anderson fairytale of *The Little Mermaid*.

The Weeki Wachee Springs State Park has its own white sandy beach, a lazy river ride, flume rides at Buccaneer Bay and plenty more action in the only spring-fed waterpark in Florida.

McKethan Lake Nature Trail

If calmer waters are what you seek, stop off at the Withlacoochee State Forest Recreation Center. It is on Hwy 41, 8 miles north of Brooksville and just south of the Citrus/Hernando County state line. The lake has a road winding around it which makes a scenic drive or a leisurely 1.5 mile walk. If you prefer to take the nature trail, the free nature trail leaflet points out 24 marked stations with points of interest from ferns and fungus to species of native trees. The circular nature trail also circumnavigates the lake and runs for 1.9 miles.

Where to Eat around Brooksville

Brooksville has several cafés offering drinks and snacks, or enjoy a picnic at one of the picnic tables overlooking lovely McKethan Lake.

Cost
Buccaneer Bay and Weeki Wachee Show Park
Adults $26, children 6-12 $12, under 6s are free

Show Park only
Adults $13, children $5, under 5s are free.

Entrance to **McKethan Lake Nature Trail**, $2 per person at the self-service pay station.

Opening Times
Opening times at Weeki Wachee Springs State Park vary, but generally the park is open Thursdays through Sundays from 10 a.m. to 3 p.m. with slightly longer opening hours during the summer. Call (352) 592-5656 or check the www.weekiwachee.com website before leaving home, to confirm opening times.

McKethan Lake, Withlacoochee State Park is open daily from 8 a.m. to dusk.

Top Tips
There are many picnic tables set out around the beautiful McKethan Lake so pack a picnic or drinks and snacks to make the most of this scenic area.

Nearby Attractions
- Cooter Pond Park, Inverness
- Webster Market

Webster Market

Most people find their way to the large Markets of Marion without the need for a guidebook, but the Webster Flea Market is a little more off the beaten track and is also a real farmer's market. The market was established in 1937 by local farmers to sell vegetables, junk and cattle. It has grown to cover an amazing 40 acres with 2,000 vendors selling almost everything you can think of. Tuesday is the cattle market sale day. It is now Florida's oldest and largest flea market, in the middle of nowhere!

Location
South of The Villages, near Bushnell

483 Northwest 1st Street
Webster
(Hwy 471 south of Sumterville)

GPS Coordinates: 28.615, -82.056

Directions from the Villages to Webster Flea Market

- From Hwy 466 head west to Oxford and turn left (south) onto Hwy 301
- Drive approximately 13½ miles then turn left at Sumterville onto Hwy 471
- Continue for about 10 miles to Webster

Just before you reach the main Webster Flea Market you will see various antiques stalls set up along the roadside, but keep going until you reach the Webster Market car park on the right. Parking is $2.

Things to Do at Webster Flea Market

Shopping, browsing, bargain hunting and people-watching pretty much covers this day out. Stalls sell belts, clothing, t-shirts, kiddies clothing, knock-off designer bags (Coach etc.), heaps of fresh local produce, nuts, weigh-outs, household items, tools, car parts, electronics, golf clubs, pets, plants, crafts, jewelry, Red Hats gear, antiques and junk too. There are ample concessions for snacks and drinks. It is probably the only place men secretly enjoy shopping as much as the ladies!

Where to Eat around Webster Flea Market

Follow your nose to find the hot food and concessions at the market – and look for the longest lines to find the best hot dogs, burgers, polish sausages, pizza, home fries with cheese and plenty of ice cream and funnel cakes too. It is certainly the cheapest place to eat out in the area and there are plenty of picnic tables around.

Cost

Admission Free. Car parking is $2

Opening Times

Mondays only. 7 a.m. to 3 p.m.

Nearby Attractions

- Lakeridge Winery
- Dade Battlefield Historic Site
- Silver Lake Recreation Area

Harry P. Leu Gardens, Orlando

The Harry P. Leu Gardens were established to inspire visitors to understand and appreciate plants, and it is easy to do so at this lovely Florida location near Orlando. The 50-acre formal gardens are centered on the restored family home and have been welcoming visitors to this beautiful retreat since 1961.

Harry P. Leu and his wife Mary Jane were garden-lovers and their successful local business in industrial supplies allowed them to travel the world, indulging in their passion of plant collecting. They brought back many exotic species and filled their garden, which overlooked the shores of Lake Rowena. Their amazing horticultural masterpiece is shared with the world today. As well as offering self-guided tours of the various themed gardens, there are half-hourly guided tours of the delightfully restored home and museum which is on the National Register of Historic Places.

Photo: VisitOrlando

Location
Northeast Orlando

Harry P. Leu Gardens
1920 N. Forest Ave
Orlando FL 32803
Tel: (407) 246-2620

GPS Coordinates: 28.568, -81.357

Directions from the Villages to Harry P. Leu Gardens

- Travel south down Hwy 441 through Leesburg and Tavares towards Orlando
- After about 60 miles turn left and go east on W. Princeton Street
- Turn right on N. Orange Ave then first left into Virginia Drive
- After one mile, follow the road as it curves to the left and take the left turn lane into the gardens

Allow 1¾ hours for the 75 mile journey.

Alternatively, for those who want to get there faster and spend longer in the gardens:

- Follow the Florida Turnpike south to exit 265 and follow Hwy 408 east
- Take exit 12A and merge with Hwy 526
- Turn left onto S. Bumby Ave, keeping right at the fork
- After 2 miles, turn left into Corrine Drive and right into N. Forest Ave

Allow 75 minutes to cover this 60 mile journey.

Things to Do at Harry P. Leu Gardens

From the entrance, begin your stroll through this horticultural paradise by following the Tropical Stream Garden, with its exotic gingers and the world's largest banana plant collection, to the Wyckoff Overlook beside Lake Rowena. The 3-acre Idea Gardens are an inspiration for those with compact courtyard gardens, showing that small can still be creative and interesting.

The brightly planted Butterfly Garden is always alive with fluttering colorful butterflies and leads on to the splendid Rose Garden, the largest formal rose garden in Florida. Other highlights at Leu Gardens are the splendid Floral Clock, the demonstration Vegetable Garden and the brilliant colors of the Annual Garden, which includes new varieties and design ideas for the home garden.

The 2,000 species of camellias with their full flower heads are the star attraction of Leu Gardens from October through March. This lovely area with its idyllic gazebo leads to the shady White Garden. Finally, enjoy the 20 minute guided tour of the beautifully furnished turn-of-the-century home of the Leu family, the Leu House Museum.

Where to Eat around Harry P. Leu Gardens

All these lovely gardens lack is an English tearoom, in my opinion!

Close to Leu Gardens is Winter Park, just 4 miles along Hwy 426 (Orange Ave). It has plenty of coffee shops, bakeries and full restaurants overlooking the park including Croissant Gourmet and the Wine Room on Park Avenue.

My favorite place to eat when I visit Leu Gardens is the Marketplace Café Restaurant at Nordstrom in the Florida Mall. It is 11 miles further south down Hwy 441 (Orange Blossom Trail). The hot ciabatta sandwiches are big enough to share and are served with French fries and a side of Nordstrom's signature olive aioli for dipping.

Cost

Admission $7 per adult.
Free admission, excluding groups, on the first Monday of every month.

Opening Times

Open daily 9 a.m. to 5 p.m.
Closed Christmas Day

Top Tips

Visit around Christmas and see the house beautifully decorated for a traditional family Christmas. As well as wreaths and decorated Christmas trees, the house featured model doll houses during my visit which were entrancing with their meticulously detailed furnishings.

Nearby Attractions

- Florida Mall
- Winter Park with its shops, restaurants and boat tours
- Lake Eola and Thornton Park, Downtown Orlando

Mount Dora

Mount Dora is a historic New England-style town with a charming collection of antique and gift shops, cafés and restaurants on the beautiful shores of Lake Dora. The town was settled in 1874. Ten years later, the arrival of the railroad made it a popular destination with tourists and it became known as a winter retreat for the wealthy to enjoy hunting, fishing and boating. Mount Dora frequently hosts craft fairs and art events when it is buzzing with visitors. It is a quaint place to visit before Christmas when it is bedecked with fairy lights.

Location
South of Eustis on Hwy 441/ SR46
Chamber of Commerce Tel: (352) 383-2165

GPS Coordinates: 28.802, -81.645

Directions from the Villages to Mount Dora

There are various scenic routes to Mount Dora, but the simplest way is to follow US 441 south and it will eventually merge with SR44 and bring you into Mount Dora.

- For a more scenic route, head north from the Villages to Hwy 42
- Turn right and follow the 42 east for about 9 miles, passing through Weirsdale along the way
- Turn right on Hwy 452 and follow the road through the pretty Florida countryside
- Turn right again on Hwy 19 and drive past picturesque Lake Eustis
- At the junction with the 441, go straight on and eventually join the Old US Hwy 441 which runs along the shores of Lake Dora into the town

Either way, the 32 mile-ish journey takes less than an hour from the Villages.

There is plenty of on-street parking and small car parks in the center of Mount Dora. However, if you fancy a gentle walk into town you can park in a quiet residential area and walk in. From North Donnelly Street drive along 7th Ave East and turn right down Tremain Street. It will bring you into Gilbert Park where there is a delightful boardwalk beside the lake and ample parking. A footpath runs from the park beside the boatyard for about ½ mile and brings you out on 3rd Ave in the heart of downtown Mount Dora.

Things to See and Do in Mount Dora

The first hotel to open in Mount Dora was the Alexander Hotel, in 1883, and is now the historic Lakeside Inn. Wealthy families built graceful mansions in Mount Dora in the late 19th century and used them as winter homes overlooking the lake. They are a delight to see today, lining the road as you approach the town. The John P. Donnelly House is well worth looking for with its historic plaque. It was built in grand Queen Anne style in 1893 by the town's first mayor and has a well-deserved place on the National Register of

Historic Places. It is located on Donnelly Avenue and is a magnificent three story home painted primrose yellow with ample white railed balconies. Look for the ornate window features and the hexagonal cupola or domed tower. The building is now used as the Freemasons Lodge.

The town is a criss-cross of quiet wide streets lined with tasteful gift shops, art galleries, and antique shops. There are plenty of cafés for sustenance and seats for people watching.

The Royellou Museum offers fascinating local history exhibits and is free admission. It also runs popular Ghost Walks around Mount Dora for a small fee.

The Mount Dora Center for the Arts is on E. 5th Avenue and has a range of exhibits by local and regional artists. In keeping with the lovely lakeshore setting, there is an Antique Boat Museum on Clayton Street.

At the bottom of the hill near the public jetty and Yacht Club, the railroad crosses the main street. The Old Railroad Station is now used by the Chamber of Commerce but alongside it are usually one or two restored railway engines with carriages. They offer various tours including lunch and dinner train trips through Florida countryside in an authentic self-propelled 1928 railway motorcar. In December they run trips to see the lights at Tavares and Eustis and on occasion the company hosts Murder Mystery Dinner Trips.

Additional Info
List of Festivals in Mount Dora
Dates vary - call (352) 383-2165 to confirm

January	Antiques Extravaganza, third weekend
February	Art Festival, first weekend
	Antiques Extravaganza, third weekend
	4-day Music Festival
March	Antique Boat Show with 150 prime wooden vessels
April	Festival of Reading
	Sailing Regatta
May	Taste of Mount Dora
July	4th of July Celebration
August	Art Car Weekend
October	Bicycle Festival, second weekend
	Craft Festival, fourth weekend
November	Plant and Garden Fair, first weekend
	Antique Extravaganza, third weekend
	Light Up Mount Dora with 2 million lights, Sunday after Thanksgiving
December	Christmas Walk, stroll with street entertainment, first Friday
	Lighted Boat Christmas Parade, first Saturday
	Christmas Tour of Homes, first weekend
	Christmas Parade down Donnelly Street

Where to Eat in Mount Dora

I have a couple of particular favorite places to eat, but you really can't go wrong at any of the establishments. The Sunshine Mountain Bakery is ideal for picking up freshly baked muffins and coffee and sitting outside in the park. It is on 3rd Avenue. A little pricier is the Windsor Rose Tea Room for afternoon tea with its very English atmosphere. For sunset drinks and dinner, grab a table on the outdoor terrace at Pisces Rising on 4th Ave and enjoy great lake views, excellent fish dishes and good service.

Nearby Attractions

- The small town of Tavares
- Boardwalk and historic bandstand at Ferran Park, right on Lake Eustis in the town of Eustis
- Lake Griffin Park in Leesburg
- Blue Spring State Park

Winter Park Scenic Boat Tour

Unbelievably, I had lived in the Villages for 6 years before I heard a whisper about this boat trip. I had to ask the Manager of the Publix in Orlando, a life-long Orlando resident, how to find it! A hidden treasure indeed and a great place to take visiting guests.

Location
Northeast Orlando

312 E Morse Blvd
Winter Park, FL 32789
Tel: (407) 644-4056

GPS Coordinates: 28.598, -81.347

Directions from the Villages to Winter Park
- Leave the Villages and follow Hwy 441 south towards Orlando for about 45 miles
- At Rosemont, head east on Hwy 423 (Lee Rd) for about 3.3 miles, passing beneath the I-4
- Turn right on N Orlando Ave (17/92)
- Shortly afterwards turn left into W. Morse Blvd and drive one mile to the very end of the road

Free parking is available at the end of the road, just before the boat dock. At the weekend you may have to park closer to the town of Winter Park where there is free parking for up to 3 hours.

Allow 1¼ hours for the 66 mile journey.

Things to Do at Winter Park
This one-hour boat trip cruises through the natural beauty of the lakes and canals around historic Winter Park in northeast Orlando. The scenic boat tour leaves the dock every day except Christmas Day. First trips are at 10 a.m. and run hourly thereafter until 4 p.m. At peak times two or three boats run, so you should easily be able to turn up and get a ride.

The pontoon boats are very stable and suitable for the shallower waters in the canals which connect the lakes, but they have no awning to protect from the sun (or the showers!) due to the low bridges. Bench seats are provided for around 18 passengers. The ticket office stands on the edge of the lake and opens before the first trip of the day just before 10 a.m. It is advisable to buy your ticket as early as possible to get a good seat. Benches under a canopy are provided whilst you wait for the boat to arrive. The boat skippers are also excellent tour narrators. They give a good patter about the sights and the wildlife, a few corny jokes and will happily answer any questions.

The boat trip begins on Lake Osceola where there are many multi-million dollar homes along the shores. After navigating through the interconnecting canal, the trip continues around Lake Virginia. The lake is shared with other boats, fishermen, jet skis and even a water-skier or two. Expect to see plenty of birds such as blue herons, which were nesting in the trees during my early-April trip. There are egrets, ducks and ducklings, anhingas, little blue herons and even osprey living in the live oaks which hang over the lake. Bougainvillea, sleeping hibiscus and plenty of bamboo add to the natural interest.

The exclusive Rollins College campus is spread along the edge of Lake Virginia with some fine buildings and it is the source of some interesting facts and anecdotes. After returning and traversing Lake Osceola along the eastern shore the boat then navigates through the winding Venetian canal and Lake Maitland opens out before you. The Kraft Azalea Park is a picture in early spring. Enjoy viewing the beautiful gardens and multi-million dollar mansions which are the winter homes of wealthy American families.

Additional Info
After a most enjoyable hour the trip ends back at the dock and you probably feel in need of refreshment. Park Avenue in Winter Park is a short walk from the lake. It is a delightful upmarket collection of shops and cafés in which to browse and dine. Across the road are the Amtrak station and a beautiful park with fountains, a heavenly scented rose garden and a pergola. This is also the location of the delightful Farmers' Market on Saturday mornings.

Where to Eat around Winter Park
Stroll along Morse Boulevard a couple of hundred yards from the boat dock towards Winter Park's charming center and you will pass Croissant Gourmet. Coffee and cold drinks, hot stuffed croissants and a delicious array of French pastries tempt you to sit at one of their indoor or curbside tables. A decadent treat, but worth it.

Just around the corner in Park Avenue there are a number of restaurants which spill onto the sidewalk, including the Bistro on Park Avenue and 310 Park South. They are all well-priced for lunch and are obviously very popular.

Cost
Boat Tour - Adults $12, children $6. Cash or Check only

Opening Times
Open daily except Christmas Day
First cruise 10 a.m. then hourly until 4 p.m.

Top Tips
- Buy your ticket early and then go for a walk around the town. When the boat is loaded, parties are called by name in the order they bought the tickets, so early ticket-buyers get to pick the best seats

- Take an 11 a.m. trip and enjoy lunch afterwards in nearby Winter Park

- Bring a sunhat and a light raincoat if showers are likely as the boats are open

Nearby Attractions
- Charles Hosmer Morse Museum of American Art in Winter Park is a collection of art including some wonderful Tiffany glass
- Mead Botanical Gardens are within a 55-acre public park just off S. Orlando Ave with paths and a boardwalk through the sub-tropical plants
- The Kraft Azalea Gardens are beautiful all year round, set along the shores of Lake Maitland
- Harry P. Leu Gardens are also a delightful day out with extensive gardens and a historic home which is open to the public

Over to You

If you have enjoyed these Days Out in Central Florida from The Villages you may want to contribute to the next book –

Favorite Days Out in Central Florida by the Villagers

If you would like to suggest your favorite day out which has not yet been covered I would love to hear your ideas. The top 15 destinations will be covered in detail and will include a photograph of the proposer and a short statement on what makes it a great day out from the Villages.

Please email the details of your favorite destination in Central Florida to me at: yourtravelgirl@gmail.com

Please include:

- Your name
- Your home Village
- Your contact details
- A sentence or two on why this is your favorite day out from the Villages

and I will do the rest.

If your suggestion is chosen to be included in the next book, you will get to see your name and photograph in print and a complimentary copy of the book, signed by the author, will be sent to you.

Bok Gardens + Grove House (p. 24) ↱ Hx of Citrus in FL
▲300 ft↑ sea level- highest in state.
Winter Park (cafe's) ; Florida Mall

    US 27, 441   Orange Blossom Trail

Edna Hibel Museum -
   Fl. Atlantic U., Jupiter

Katherin Rawlings - novels of central FL, eg Sumter Ctg NW,
+ N.E Lake Crty. per, Andrew Blechman's Leisureville

Coming Soon

Look out for more books by Gillian Birch in this popular series:

- Days Out in Central Florida

- Days Out in Central Florida with Children

- Days Out in Central Florida for Active Seniors

- Favorite Days Out in Central Florida by the Villagers

- Free Things to Do in Orlando

These will shortly be available in paperback from Amazon.com and your local bookstore and will also be available as ebooks

You can also keep up with future publications on my website: www.gillianbirch.com

If you have enjoyed this book please post a review on Amazon.com

http://amzn.to/Quwlh3 Thank you.

ABOUT THE AUTHOR

Gillian Birch is a freelance travel writer and, whenever possible between trips, she is a resident of The Villages. As the wife of a Master Mariner, she has traveled extensively and lived in some exotic locations all over the world, including Europe, the Far East and the Republic of Panama. Her love of writing meant she kept detailed journals which are a valuable source of eye-witness information for her many published magazine articles and destination reviews.

Describing herself as having "endless itchy feet and an insatiable wanderlust", she continues to explore Florida and further afield with her husband, writing about her experiences with wonderful clarity and attention to detail.

She has a Diploma from the British College of Journalism and is proud to be a member of the International Travel Writers' Alliance and the Florida Writers' Association. Learn more about her writing as YourTravelGirl at www.gillianbirch.com

Made in the USA
Middletown, DE
07 May 2015